THE

GHOSTLY TALES

OF

SANTA FE

Published by Arcadia Children's Books
A Division of Arcadia Publishing
Charleston, SC
www.arcadiapublishing.com

Spooky America is a trademark of Arcadia Publishing, Inc.

First published 2023

Manufactured in the United States

ISBN 978-1-4671-9734-2

Library of Congress Control Number: 2023931845

All images used courtesy of Shutterstock.com; p. 42 Andriy Blokhin/Shutterstock.com.

Notice: The information in this book is true and complete to the best of our knowledge. It is offered without guarantee on the part of the author or Arcadia Publishing. The author and Arcadia Publishing disclaim all liability in connection with the use of this book.

Spooky America

THE
GHOSTLY TALES
OF
SANTA FE

LISHA CAUTHEN

Adapted from *Haunted Santa Fe* by Ray John de Aragón

arcadia
CHILDREN'S BOOKS

UTAH

COLORADO

ARIZONA

NEW MEXICO

TEXAS

SANTA FE

Table of Contents & Map Key

Welcome to Spooky Santa Fe!

Imagine hauling freight across the Santa Fe Trail in the 1800s. You are hot. You are thirsty. You are covered in dust.

You started in Independence, Missouri, two and a half months ago, driving a team of oxen pulling a Conestoga wagon nine hundred miles across the prairie. You endured blazing sun, poisoned water holes, and a cruel wagon master. One of your friends was left behind, buried on the trail, dead from a rattlesnake bite.

Now, you are at the end of the trail.

You are in Santa Fe, New Mexico.

You arrive in the Plaza, the center of this city established in 1610 as *La Villa Real de la Santa Fé de San Francisco de Asís* (The Royal Town of the Holy Faith of Saint Francis of Assisi). The Plaza was built on the ruins of an abandoned pueblo called *Oghá P'o'oge* (translated as "white shell water place"), which was built by the Tewa tribe.

After spending so much time on the featureless prairie, and then, the parched desert, the crowded Plaza is overwhelming. Everywhere you turn, you see colorful carts full of squash and corn creaking over the rutted streets, farmers transporting complaining livestock, armed soldiers in their impressive uniforms, insistent traders shouting to the crowd to come buy their goods, and hard-working townsfolk trying to serve them all. Indigenous peoples, Spanish soldiers and settlers, and immigrants from all over the world congregate in Santa Fe. The sight

of the enormous Palace of the Governors, built in 1610, the Presidio that houses the battle-hardened soldiers, and the bustling stores fills you with awe.

But you are thirsty.

There's a trading post that has a well brimming with sweet, fresh water. Once you and your oxen quench your thirst, you are ready to sell the goods you brought all this way: bolts of silk and cotton cloth, tools, and medicine. You will return to Missouri with your wagon laden with Spanish silver, trappers' furs, and Pueblo pottery.

Much has changed in Santa Fe since its founding more than four hundred years ago, but some things have stayed the same. The Palace of the Governors still stands. It is the oldest public building in the United States. Not far from the Plaza on De Vargas Street, you will find the Oldest House in the United States. And the well where so many travelers on the Santa Fe Trail satisfied their thirst still remains in the foundation of the Original Trading Post on West San Francisco Street.

Santa Fe is still a cosmopolitan city full of shop owners, artists, and tradesmen. But not all of them are *alive*, or even, human. So when you're feeling brave enough, turn the page, and learn about the spooks and spirits that call Santa Fe home.

Koko and Coco

When the Spanish came to New Mexico in the 1500s, they brought their beliefs and stories with them. And the Pueblo peoples had beliefs of their own. Often, these world views clashed, but sometimes, they were surprisingly similar. After all, supernatural beings do not care where you come from or what you believe. Their job is to frighten you. And when you visit Santa Fe, you will find out they are very good at it.

The Spanish brought their Catholic religion to the New World, but they were also mindful of their old-world folklore. A favorite tradition concerns a monster named El Coco.

El Coco comes from the otherworld, the Land of the Dead. El Coco is a ghost-monster that snatches misbehaving children away from their parents. He lurks on rooftops, searching out naughty children who he can kidnap—and sometimes eat! Spanish parents often warn, "*¡Aquí viene El Coco!*" which means, "Here comes the Coco!" The parents sing lullabies and recite rhymes that warn their children to be good, or El Coco will spirit them away.

The Pueblo peoples also have a rich tradition concerning the unseen world, and to them, the Spirit Land is close and accessible. There are several ways to cross over into the Spirit Land.

One way is to travel during a blizzard and

wade into the Lake of Death. Whether the wanderer enters the Lake of Death by accident or on purpose, he will be sucked under the dark waters and then spit out into the bright light of the Spirit Land. Another method is to sing a song to attract a Song Hunter. Song Hunters ride sunbeams, and they search out singers to bring back to the Spirit Land. Or a seeker can follow the Road of the Dead, which is lined with mourners who clutch at those passing by. If you can avoid their grasps, you will make it to the sunny Spirit Land.

In between here and the Spirit Land lies the middle place, known as the City of Mists. Various spirits and monsters live there. Surprisingly, one of these monsters is also called the Koko.

The Pueblo peoples' Koko is said to live near Santa Fe in a hidden cave in La Sangre de Cristo Mountains (which translates as the Blood of

Christ Mountains), where it can come and go between this world, the City of Mists, and the Spirit Land. It spends eternity searching out and defeating the wicked.

According to legend, the Koko is as dark as the darkest recesses of its cave. Its skin is scaly and clammy, and its feet are webbed. The Koko is silent—it can creep up on you without a sound and kidnap you, and you will never be seen again. It hunts for its victims at night, so if you see a pair of eyes glowing in the darkness, beware! Those eyes might belong to an owl, or

they might belong to the Koko, who is looking for someone to devour.

Few have seen the Koko and lived to tell the tale, but those who have seen it describe the monster as having a curled tail, bat ears, and six fingers on each hand. Dressed in tree bark and rushes, it may crouch when it walks, or it may crawl along the ground like a lizard, changing its skin color to match its surroundings. Rocks bruise the Koko's webbed feet, so it often wears sandals it has woven from yucca leaves. With all the bad people in the world, the Koko has a lot of prey to choose from. It never rests.

To this day, the Koko is said to still roam the streets of Santa Fe. As one elder storyteller explains, one sunny winter afternoon, a band of Pueblo warriors was hunting in the mountains. Prey was scarce that day, and they wandered farther into the wilderness than usual. As night fell, they realized they were lost.

The warriors decided to spend the night in an abandoned Tewa village. As they huddled together for warmth and safety, they heard strange noises. Was it an animal? Was it a ghost? They strained their eyes, searching the darkness, then saw a light bouncing among the trees.

Suddenly, the creature appeared. It was the Koko! The light the warriors had seen was coming from the monster's magical head. Flames flickered in the Koko's face where its eyes, nose, and mouth should have been. To their horror, the Koko's head then flew off its body, circling and teasing the warriors.

Normally, the warriors were brave, but they were no match for the Koko. They were terrified. They shot all their arrows into the supernatural beast, but none had any effect.

When the beast was upon them, the warriors begged for mercy. The Koko was moved by their woeful cries and took pity on them. He struck a bargain. The Koko would let them go if they paid him tribute every year by carving his terrible face into pumpkins, lighting a small fire inside them, and placing the pumpkins on wooden poles around the village. The warriors eagerly agreed. To this day, members of the Tewa tribe perform a ritual dance and carve pumpkins to honor the Koko.

The Koko's cave is near Santa Fe, so the town is its favored hunting ground. If you walk the streets late at night in Santa Fe, watch out for those glowing eyes. Or a fiery pumpkin head. Because if you have not been as good as you can be, the Koko may be looking for you.

San Miguel Church

A Day of Tears

Although the world views of the Spanish and the Pueblo peoples often clashed, for more than a century, the colonists and indigenous tribes largely lived in harmony. However, the differences came to a boiling point in 1680, when the Pueblo people united against the Spanish colonists. This event in Santa Fe history is called the Pueblo Revolt. Many people suffered and died throughout the area during the uprising, and not all seem to have passed on to the other side.

The Spanish protected the Pueblo people from Apache and Navajo raids. They brought European livestock like cows, horses, and pigs and crops like wheat, cabbage, and peaches to Pueblo farmers. However, for the Spanish, the most important thing they brought to the New World was their Catholic faith.

The Spanish expected the Pueblo peoples to abandon their customs and their religious beliefs. Some converted to the new, Spanish religion and helped build churches; however, most did not.

Pueblo spiritual leaders held religious ceremonies in kivas, which are chambers built fully or partially underground. Some of them practiced rituals to communicate with deities, or gods, that could help them foretell the future, cure pandemics, and even levitate, which means to hover in the air. The Spanish were uncomfortable with Pueblo religious practices, and they restricted the masks, dances, and rituals that the Pueblo peoples had used for thousands of years.

Over time, resentment between the groups grew. The area suffered a serious drought, and the Pueblo peoples lost crops. Little by little, the wildlife they hunted disappeared. When the Pueblo peoples decided to rise up, the churches and the Franciscan priests were their first targets.

The final event that broke the relationship between the Spanish and the Pueblo peoples occurred in 1675. Spanish soldiers arrested four Pueblo men for practicing witchcraft. The men were not witches, they simply resisted converting to Catholicism. They wanted to continue worshiping in their own way.

They thought the drought, crop failures, and disappearing wild game were punishment for abandoning their ancient ways, and they wanted to make amends with the spirit world. Though the governor was eventually forced to release the four men, the trust between the Pueblo peoples and the Spanish was severed.

One of these men was named Po'pay. The Spanish had whipped him in the Santa Fe Plaza for practicing witchcraft, and he never forgot it. After his release, he moved to a remote community tucked in the Sangre de Cristo mountains, Taos Pueblo, where he performed ceremonies in a kiva. He had a vision.

Several fearsome Pueblo spirits appeared to him in the flickering shadows of his ceremonial fire. According to Po'pay, the spirits said the reason the rains didn't come and the land died was because the Pueblo peoples were not allowed to dance their sacred dances. Po'pay said these spirits told him to unite the Pueblo peoples and rebel against the Spanish. If the Pueblo peoples drove out the Spanish, destroyed everything the Spanish had brought them, and returned to the old ways, the rains would come again, and the spirits would bless the Pueblo peoples with prosperity.

The Pueblo peoples were not one tribe— they belonged to many self-governing indigenous communities like the Tewa, Hopi, Acoma, Zuni, and Taos. Po'pay sent messengers to all the communities. The messengers carried yucca ropes with knots tied in them. Each knot represented one day. The communities were instructed to untie one knot every day. When they untied the last knot, it was time to attack the Spanish. Some of the Pueblo communities and Pueblo Catholic converts did not participate in the revolt—they were attacked too.

On Saturday, August 10, 1680, the Catholic priests, colonists, and Pueblo peoples who had converted to Catholicism gathered in their churches to celebrate St. Lorenzo Day. That day, the Pueblo communities untied the last knot in their ropes, and at dawn, they attacked.

First, they attacked the churches in their own communities. They killed priests and Catholic worshippers, and burned churches, buildings, and crops. Livestock and other animals were also killed. Then they followed the fleeing survivors to Santa Fe.

The Spanish colonists barricaded themselves in the Palace of the Governors, but they soon ran out of supplies. The Pueblo peoples had dammed the river, denying water to the town.

Eventually, the Spanish gave up, and two thousand survivors fled south to El Paso del Norte, now called El Paso, Texas.

About six hundred settlers and twenty-two Franciscan priests were killed in the revolt. If you walk past the Palace of the Governors on a still night, you may hear the ghostly wails and weeping of the trapped Spanish colonists echoing in the Plaza. And if you take the time to light a candle at San Miguel Church, you may hear the whispers of the dead victims, some of whose bones still lie on the church grounds.

We do not know how many Pueblo peoples died in the revolt, but we do know that Po'pay led his people back to their ancient ways. He demanded

that the Pueblo peoples return to their native names. He wanted them to destroy all the Catholic religious items, like tabernacles, bells, crosses, rosaries, and entire churches. Po'pay wanted to eliminate everything that reminded them of the Spanish.

Even though the Pueblo peoples returned to their masked Kachina dances and ancient rituals, the rains did not come. The Apache and Navajo still terrorized the Pueblo peoples. The native crops failed. The wild game did not return. After a year of Po'pay's severe rule, he was overthrown, and no one knows what happened to him.

Twelve years after the survivors of the Pueblo Revolt escaped to El Paso, the Spanish returned to the territory. But things between the Pueblo peoples and the Spanish were different. The Spanish allowed them to use their kivas and perform their sacred dances.

However, the ghosts of those who lost their lives during the Pueblo Revolt are still restless, and if you want to glimpse a phantom specter, visit during the fall Fiestas de Santa Fe, which honors the return of the Spanish. On the last day of the celebration, a solemn Catholic Mass is held at the Cathedral Basilica of Saint

Francis of Assisi. At the end of the Mass, the participants join a haunting candlelight procession that winds its way for about a half-mile through the old Santa Fe streets.

Light your candle and join the walk, which ends at the Cross of the Martyrs on Martyrs Hill. On the top of the hill, you will see small bonfires and luminarias, which are brown paper bags half-filled with sand and lit with glowing votive candles. Martyrs Hill is the spot where several priests and members of their church temporarily escaped the bloodshed during the revolt by running away, up the hill. But they were not safe. As they knelt in prayer, their attackers massacred all of them.

As you listen to the prayers for the dead, cup your hand around your candle flame, peer into the darkness, and listen carefully. Many have reported hearing the cries and prayers of those kneeling priests and church members killed so long ago. Flickering lights are seen when no one is there, and shadowy figures pass close by. Are they the ghosts of the priests? Or perhaps they are the souls of the Spanish and Pueblo peoples, still fighting for their culture? You may even see the hooded figure of a Franciscan priest dressed in his traditional brown robes, fleeing from the church, reliving that bloody, fateful day in 1680.

De Vargas Street House

Brujas and Brujos

The soldier's sword was heavy, but his heart was heavier. He trudged up the winding, dark street that ended at the oldest house in town, the house of the two sisters. He would do anything to achieve his heart's desire, even face two *brujas*.

In New Mexico, female witches are known as *brujas* and male witches are known as *brujos*. *Brujas* and *brujos* are said to have special powers. They know things. They may talk with the dead or inhuman spirits, or they may foretell the future. Old Santa Fe lore advises townspeople to put a cap on their chimneys when they are not being used to keep out the *brujas* and *brujos*. However, even though people are afraid of them, they may visit a *bruja* or *brujo* for help when they are desperate. Have you ever been so desperate that you would ask for help from a witch?

The De Vargas Street House is also known as the Oldest House because, according to the stories, it is the oldest continuously occupied house in the United States. No one knows when the house was first built, but it was long before the Spanish ever came to Santa Fe. The foundations are said to have been laid by Pueblo peoples, perhaps as early as the 1200s. The Spanish added to the abandoned dwelling and used it to house new settlers.

For a time, a strange pair of sisters lived in the Oldest House. They were *brujas*. The townspeople respected and feared them. Mostly, the townspeople stayed out of their way. But on a clear, quiet night, a desperate Spanish soldier knocked on the *brujas'* door.

The soldier was hopelessly in love with a girl who did not love him back. He would do anything to make the girl love him—even ask the *brujas* for help. He paid the *brujas* to mix a love potion and cast a spell that would make the girl love him. With the help of the *brujas'* magic, he was confident his object of affection would love him back.

But magic is not reliable. Or maybe the *brujas* did not intend to help the soldier. Maybe they wanted to trick him. Whatever the reason, the love potion did not work. The love spell did not work. The girl did not love the soldier, and the soldier was angry. He rode his pony back to the Oldest House and pounded on the door. He demanded the *brujas* give him his money back.

But it is not wise to be angry at witches. After a violent argument, the *brujas* cut off the soldier's head and tossed it down the street.

If you are brave enough, pass by the Oldest House on De Vargas Street on a full-moon night. You may hear the sighs of the heartsick soldier as he knocks on the *brujas'* door. Or, more likely, you may see the Headless Horseman of Santa Fe racing by on his snorting pony, in search of his missing head.

Across the street from the Oldest House stands San Miguel Church. San Miguel Church is the oldest church in the continental United States. Some sense restless spirits in and around the church. They hear ancient voices murmur or feel the slight draft of a wraith, which is a wispy shadow of a spirit, passing nearby. The church was built in 1610 on top of a kiva and many unmarked graves are buried on the grounds. One of those graves is said to belong to a famous Santa Fe witch who lived in the mid-1800s: El Brujo Teofilo.

Teofilo was an ordinary child and teenager. But a terrible trauma awakened his sleeping powers. When Teofilo was eighteen, he was traveling the *Jornada del Muerto*, which means the Journey of the Dead Man. The *Jornada del Muerto* is a dangerous and desolate desert area. There, a band of Apaches captured Teofilo. They laid him on the ground, staked his arms and legs with wet leather strips, and poured sweet powder in his mouth. Then they left him in the hot sun.

As the leather strips dried, they shrank and pulled Teofilo's arms and legs farther and farther apart. He felt as though he would be torn wide open. The sweet powder the Apaches

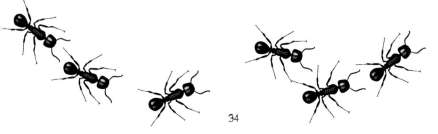

poured in his mouth attracted ants. Teofilo kept his mouth shut, but the ants still swarmed him, crawling into his eyes and biting his face and body. Teofilo thought he was done for.

Suddenly, Teofilo felt surprisingly calm. In his mind, he saw a soaring vulture. Somehow, he thought about the vulture so much that he *became* the vulture and flew away from his torturous predicament.

Teofilo was having a spiritual experience, like many holy men and *brujos* do. As the vulture, he flew across the landscape and saw a dead deer that had been attacked by coyotes. He thought so hard about the dead deer that the ants seemed to hear his thoughts. They left

him and went looking for the fresh-killed deer to feast on.

Teofilo found himself back on the ground, watching a real vulture swoop toward him. The vulture landed beside him and began to peck at Teofilo's arm.

But Teofilo did not panic. He closed his eyes, slowed his breath, concentrated on his spread-out arms, and felt himself rise. Suddenly, he *became* an eagle, soaring high overhead. He thought about the leather straps that bound his body, which were made of jackrabbit hide. He thought about the jackrabbit straps so hard that the vulture heard his thoughts. The vulture turned its attention to pecking at the leather straps instead of Teofilo's arm, and soon, Teofilo was free.

Teofilo stood. His eyes were so dry he had to rub them with something wet, but the only liquid he had was the blood flowing from the gash in his arm. It would have to do. Teofilo rubbed his own blood in his eyes, and something strange happened.

He could see everything, but not with his eyes—he was seeing the world through the vulture's eyes.

He saw the whole ravine for miles and miles, and all that was in it. He saw every lizard hiding under every rock. He saw a water spring around the bend where he could quench his thirst. And he knew that a group of soldiers from Santa Fe would soon appear over the horizon to save him.

No one knows why Teofilo's suffering gave him such powers, but from that time on, he could foretell the future. He knew what people were thinking. Sometimes, he was able to move from place to place without being seen—the people in town would be startled when Teofilo would simply rise up mysteriously from the ground in front of them.

At first, he used his new, amazing powers for good. But over time, Teofilo slowly stopped worshiping God. He stopped going to Mass and blessing himself with holy water. He began to believe that he, not God, had power over life and death.

All that changed one day when his friend's daughter, Emilia, was playing fetch with her dog in a field. Emilia threw the ball too far, and it bounced into the rushing, swollen river nearby. The dog jumped in the river to retrieve the ball, but the water was too rough. Emilia, alarmed, jumped in to save him.

Soon they were both in trouble. Townspeople saw the pair fighting the water and pulled them out, but for Emilia, it was too late. She had inhaled too much water into her lungs and drowned.

Teofilo was on the other side of town but somehow, he knew what had happened. He hurried to the river and picked up Emilia's limp body. For the first time in a long time, he admitted that only God had power over life and death. Teofilo prayed and sang to the angels to help him. He imagined Emilia alive and well, and he imagined himself becoming one with the earth.

The townspeople cautiously approached and found Emilia standing next to Teofilo's still body. His prayers were answered—Emilia was alive! But Teofilo had given his life for hers.

Though there is no tombstone for Teofilo, you can be sure that he is buried on the grounds of San Miguel Church. If you want to meet Teofilo yourself, visit the church grounds

early in the morning, when only the birds are stirring. Walk around the ancient building—but be alert. Do not be startled when Teofilo simply rises up mysteriously from the ground to greet you.

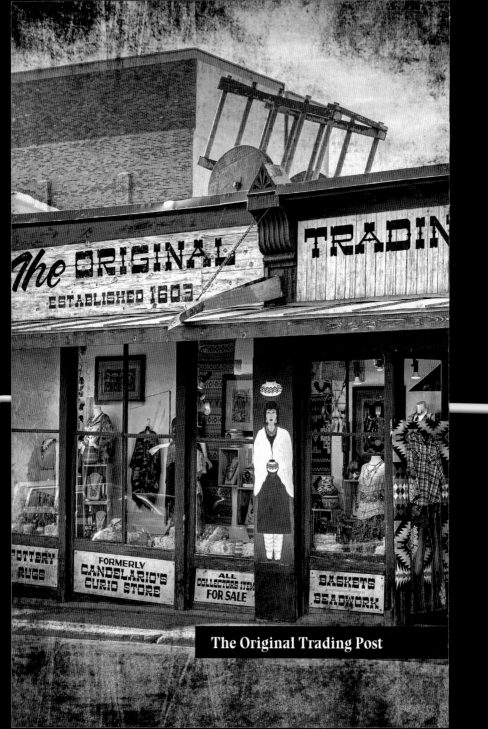

The Original Trading Post

Curios and
Treasures

How can you find a haunted location? Look for
a building with a long history, where people
from all over the world have crossed paths. A
space where strange, exotic items have been
bought and sold for centuries. These spots
echo with the whispers of the long-dead
as they eternally relive their triumphs and
disappointments.

The Original Trading Post, located on West San Francisco Street, is such a place. It is said that the site existed before the Spanish colonists arrived. The first trading post was a tent, which was set up on the site in 1603. The building you see today is built on four-hundred-year-old foundations that include a well that quenched the thirst of countless travelers on the Santa Fe Trail. As you walk the wooden floors of the trading post, stop and listen. Did the floor creak? Was it the

spirit of a long-dead peddler bringing wares to sell? Do you hear voices from across the past, haggling and striking deals? One of the many people who traded and sold goods on this site was Jesus S. Candelario.

Jesus S. Candelario's father was an early trader who sent goods along the Santa Fe Trail to the United States. As a boy, Candelario traveled with his father across the plains, trading with the Comanches. When he grew up, he took over the family business and founded the Old Curio Store. A curio is an item that is uncommon, rare, and interesting. People buy curios to own something unusual and fascinate their family and friends.

Candelario paid Pueblo artisans to make pottery, blankets, and turquoise jewelry for his store. He bought folk art from tinsmiths and carpenters. Sometimes, mysterious people brought him ancient amulets and statues of strange beings they had found in the desert or in the mountains. Many of the items Candelario bought were of such high quality, they are housed in museums today.

Candelario was a champion of Santa Fe. He loved his city and wanted everyone else to love it, too. He also understood that money could be made from tourism. So, he lured people to come out West by selling some of the first postcards ever printed. They were made from photographs of historic buildings and local Pueblo peoples. Anyone who wanted an adventure would come to Santa Fe. And when they came, they stopped at the Old Curio Store to buy souvenirs and see the many interesting people who hung out there. One of these people was El Ciego, a name that means the blind one.

El Ciego was devoted to attending Mass at San Miguel Church every day. One day, El Ciego was at church when the tower bell rang all on its own, with no one pulling the toll rope. El Ciego had been blind, but suddenly, he could see! Tears ran down his face as he looked at the flickering candles, the glinting crucifix, the worshippers in their colorful clothes, and the priest saying Mass. El Ciego finished his prayers and joyously ran to tell his friends and family what had happened. But he discovered that once he'd left the church, he was blind again.

Strangely, the next day when El Ciego went to Mass, the bell rang all on its own again. And again, El Ciego could see. It seems that whenever the bell rang while El Ciego was in the church, he could see. When he left the church, his sight was gone. He accepted this gift with joy and spent many days at Candelario's Old Curio Store, testifying to the miracle of his temporary sight. Some say he is there still, and if you listen carefully, you may hear El Ciego's creaking rocking chair as he testifies to the miracle of his temporary sight.

Some of the curios Candelario bought came from treasure hunters. During the Pueblo Revolt in 1680, many Spanish colonists buried their valuables in caves before they fled. They planned to dig them up when they returned—

but not everyone returned. Or maybe they couldn't remember where they buried their precious things. By the early 1900s, rumors of secret maps leading to untold riches circulated around the territory. One story tells of a large, solid-silver railing removed from a church and hidden in the mountains. The silver railing has still not been found.

One day, a man came to the Old Curio Store and told Candelario a fantastic tale. The man had been hunting game in the Sangre de Cristo Mountains. As he'd passed a certain cave, he noticed something glinting in the sun. The man looked in and saw Spanish armor, chests, and church relics made of gold and silver. The man was afraid a wild animal lived in the shadows, so he didn't venture very far inside the cave. Instead, he used some brush and branches to hide the entrance, identified several landmarks so he could find the treasure cave again, and came to Candelario for help.

Candelario knew the man. He decided the man was telling the truth. So, he gave him ropes, picks and shovels, torches, a horse, and some mules to carry back the treasure.

Days went by. Then, weeks. Finally, the

man returned. He told Candelario that he had hidden the cave so well, even *he* couldn't find it! He had become confused looking for the landmarks he had identified—so many trees, rocks, and outcroppings looked like the trees, rocks, and outcroppings he had seen near the treasure cave. The unfortunate man decided to keep looking. He wandered the Sangre de Cristo Mountains for the rest of his days, searching for the lost riches. Some say his fruitless search drove him mad and his spirit is still out there looking.

What would you do if you couldn't find your treasure cave? Would you give up? Or would you keep looking? If you do go on your own

treasure hunt, perhaps looking for that missing silver railing, keep an eye out. You may meet the poor man's spirit in the Sangre de Cristo

Mountains as he desperately looks for the right trees, rocks, and outcroppings that mark his cave. Maybe you will hear the plodding of his pack mules as they patiently accompany him on his search. Or, if you're lucky, when you visit the Original Trading Post to buy your own souvenir curio or send a postcard, you may spy the shadow of the doomed man as he hurries through the store to tell Candelario his story.

Raids, Battles, and Wars

One of the first structures built in Santa Fe was the Presidio. The Presidio was a compound of military buildings that housed over one hundred Spanish soldiers and their horses near the Palace of the Governors. Thousands of Spanish soldiers protected the citizens while Spain owned the territory. In 1822, Mexico took possession of the land and put Mexican soldiers in charge of defending it. In 1846, many battles were fought and the U.S. Army ultimately captured Santa Fe. The lives and deaths of the soldiers who fought have left their mark. Though the Presidio is now gone, some visitors are certain many soldiers have never left.

When you visit the Plaza, eat a delicious New Mexican meal of chiles rellenos or carne adovada at one of the local restaurants. Then stroll the historic lanes and alleys. You may hear strange sounds like the rattle of swords or the clatter of boots on cobblestone. Many believe they've heard Spanish soldiers march home to the Presidio on these old streets, returning from battle.

The Spanish soldiers were called *soldados de cuera*, or leather soldiers. They wore leggings made of leather and carried leather shields to protect them from Indigenous peoples' arrows. The soldiers fought many fierce battles over the centuries. One particularly bloody battle happened in 1779. Juan José Chavez and around five hundred Presidio soldiers were called upon to stop nearly a thousand or more Comanche from terrorizing the frontier. The soldiers joined Ute, Apache, and Pueblo allies and traveled down the Rio Grande and Chama rivers, through mountains, and into Colorado territory. There, they launched a surprise attack on the Comanche.

The Comanche were fierce foes. They rode Spanish horses they had stolen in raids. They had guns they had captured from colonists. Cuerno Verde, which means Green Horn, is the Spanish name given to Tavibo Naritgant, chief of the Comanche. He wore a distinctive leather headdress with a green-painted animal horn attached.

The fight was difficult and bloody. The Comanche were brave, daring, and ruthless in battle. The Spanish soldiers were equally ferocious. The Comanches had gained the upper hand, and the Spanish soldiers and their allies feared defeat. Suddenly, Juan José Chavez realized he was behind Cuerno Verde on his horse. Chavez spurred his horse forward and knocked Cuerno Verde to the ground. Chavez then leapt off his horse, drew his short sword, and plunged it into Cuerno Verde. Once the Comanches realized their chief was dead, they surrendered.

All the soldiers marched back to the Presidio in Santa Fe, including Juan José Chavez. Once home, Chavez expected great honors and awards for killing Cuerno Verde. But to his surprise, everyone ignored him.

He took a walk around the Plaza. He tipped his hat to ladies and bowed to gentlemen he met, but none of them returned the greeting. Why was everyone ignoring this hero who had fought so bravely? Well, you see, Chavez himself was dead and he didn't know it. He had died in that battle with the Comanches in the Colorado territory.

To this day, Chavez still does not know he is dead. As you walk home from your dinner on the Plaza, you may meet a man dressed in leather leggings, carrying a leather shield. It

is the ghost of Chavez, still searching for the honor he never received.

The American Civil War came to the New Mexico Territory in 1862. The Confederacy wanted to conquer and claim the area. If the South controlled New Mexico, it could also control the gold fields in Colorado and the trade in California. The money that flowed to the United States over the Santa Fe Trail would go to the Confederacy, and the Union economy would collapse.

The Confederates thought it would be easy to take New Mexico because most of the regular U.S. Army soldiers stationed in the territory had been called to serve elsewhere in the Civil War. But the Confederates underestimated the local farmers, ranchers, and businessmen who knew how to fight.

The U.S. Army called up Colonel John Slough from Colorado, even though he was not experienced in warfare. He was cruel to his troops and merciless to his foes. He force-marched his exhausted Colorado troops to Fort Union, New Mexico. There, he disobeyed direct orders to stay at the fort. He gathered the troops at the fort with his Colorado troops and attacked the Confederates at Glorieta, a mountain pass south of Santa Fe in the Sangre de Cristo Mountains.

The terrain was difficult—the area was surrounded by cliffs. A heavy snow fell. The battle did not go well for Slough and his men. Many died in the fierce fighting. Gravediggers had trouble digging in the frozen ground. They did their best to gather severed limbs and mangled bodies and lay them to rest, but the scene was horrific.

When all seemed lost, Lieutenant Colonel Manuel Antonio Chávez stepped in. He was known as El Leoncito, which means the Little Lion, because of his fierce fights with raiding Indigenous peoples. He arrived at Glorieta with five hundred experienced Hispanic troops—many who were former Presidio soldiers in Santa Fe. Chávez sent out Hispanic couriers and Indigenous scouts to find the enemy positions. And he came up with a plan. He and his troops would destroy the Confederates' supply lines.

The Confederate supplies were being guarded at the top of the bluffs that surrounded the battlefield. Chávez and his men took all the ropes they could find and carefully climbed the steep cliffs. The snow muffled the noise of their ascent, and they took the Confederates by surprise. Chávez burned their supply wagons and spiked their cannons. Explosions rocked the valley. The U.S. Union Army had won. But it was no thanks to Slough, who was supposed to be in charge—Chávez was the hero of the battle.

The Glorieta battlefield is about twenty miles away from Santa Fe, and it is a popular camping site. Today, campers in the area around Glorieta claim to hear the shouts and pained screams of the dying soldiers

who fought so valiantly to preserve the Union. Some have seen a phantom priest gallop past them on a snow-white horse, shouting directions toward safety in Spanish.

If you decide to camp under a starry New Mexican sky, will you welcome the battle-weary soldier when he appears in the circle of your firelight? All he desires are directions back to his home in Santa Fe, but don't be surprised when he disappears into thin air. After you spend a restless night, peer out from your tent flap into the misty morning and salute the ghost riders you may see as they travel toward their glory.

After the unnecessarily bloody battle, Slough was afraid the U.S. Army would charge him with war crimes, accuse him of disobeying orders, and blame him for all the dead U.S. Army soldiers at Glorieta. So, he resigned.

In time, however, he began to think of himself as a hero. He fooled President Andrew Johnson into thinking he was a great man. President Johnson appointed Slough as chief justice of the New Mexico Territory Supreme Court. But people in New Mexico knew that Slough was no hero. He was incompetent. He was a coward. And he spent all his time gambling and drinking at the Exchange Hotel in Santa Fe.

William Logan Rynerson, a former captain in the Civil War and a member of the New Mexico Territorial Legislature, introduced a petition to oust Slough. Slough slandered Rynerson in public, and the two had an argument at the Exchange Hotel. Rynerson pointed a gun at Slough. He demanded that Slough admit he had lied.

"Take it back," said Rynerson.

"Shoot and be damned!" said Slough.

So Rynerson shot. Slough died two days later.

Slough enjoyed gambling and drinking at the Exchange Hotel so much, he never left. The Exchange Hotel has been gone for one hundred years, but today, the La Fonda Hotel stands in the same spot. When you spend the night, you might have a hard time getting on the elevator.

It seems to go up and down on its own—but most people believe it is being operated by the specter of John Slough, coming down to the bar for another drink. If you hear a knock on the door to your room, use the peep hole to make sure someone is there—that is, someone you can see. Slough is said to knock on guests' doors as he paces the corridor. Many people have seen him roaming the halls in his long, black coat. If you happen to see his shadowy ghost, look closely. You may see a hole in his coat from the fatal bullet.

Sorrow and Joy—the Women of Santa Fe

Dates, facts, and battles are recorded in the history books. But the sorrows and joys that women faced are often told in legends. Sometimes, their stories are kept alive by the ghosts of the women themselves.

One famous woman-ghost is La Llorona, which means weeping woman. La Llorona was once a beautiful woman named Luisa, who was a maid for a rich and powerful family in

Santa Fe. Luisa went to the local dances, which were called fandangos, and met a handsome captain from the Presidio. She fell in love. Over time, Luisa had two children with the captain.

One day, Luisa was washing the clothes of the family she worked for at the Santa Fe River. Today, the river is often dry, but in the past, it was a broad, meandering channel of water. Luisa's two children waded nearby, tossing rocks in the water and trying to catch little fishes. Luisa had a lot on her mind. She had heard a rumor that the captain she loved was going to marry someone richer and more important than she was.

While Luisa was thinking about this heartbreaking gossip, a torrential rain suddenly hit the Sangre de Cristo Mountains. The water rushed down the mountains and into the Santa Fe River. In an instant, the calm water became a raging flood, and Luisa's two children were swept away. The children cried out to their mother—Luisa jumped into the river to save them, but she could not. Luisa and her children drowned.

If you hike along the riverbed, you may hear La Llorona's tormented cries echo across the valley as she pleads for her children's safety. But if you see her, run the other direction.

La Llorona has been known to mistake unwary children as her own, and she may steal you away.

Another Santa Fe woman with a sad story is Julia Staab. Julia was the young bride of Abraham Staab, a successful German Jewish immigrant who had built a thriving business in Santa Fe. Julia and Abraham had seven children and became important people in the community.

Abraham built Julia an enormous mansion. Shortly after they moved in, Julia gave birth to her eighth child. But this child did not live long. The baby died unexpectedly, and Julia went into a deep depression. Some say her hair turned white overnight.

Julia barely left her room. She barely ate. She barely slept. Julia mourned the death of her baby for three years before she, too, died. Some say she killed herself. Some say her husband murdered her. Probably, she simply wasted away.

Many years later, Julia's mansion was renovated. Today it is La Posada de Santa Fe, a luxury hotel just steps from the Historic Plaza. And though Julia had a tragic end to her life, it seems she still loves her home because she has never left. Check into La Posada and you may be in for a spooky experience.

As you sign in at the desk, keep a close eye on the lobby—Julia is known to appear in her black, Victorian dress, still mourning her dead baby. And if the night gets cold, don't worry. Julia is known to fix the broken furnace and adjust the gas jets in the fireplace.

Glasses fly off shelves, objects move on their own, and bright orbs dance on the stairs. Orbs are balls of light, which are thought to be the manifestation of energy. They are often seen in photos but sometimes, they are seen in person. Though La Posada is a great place to work, many unnerved employees have quit after having phantom encounters.

How brave are *you*? Are you bold enough to sleep in Julia's bedroom? If you are, book a night in room 256, also called suite 100. It is on the second floor of the hotel, which still has some of the original and grand Staab family furnishings.

While you sleep, keep one ear tuned to the bathroom. You may hear the water running—taking a long, hot bath was one of Julia's favorite pastimes. And it still is. If you doze off, don't be startled when the sound of heavy breathing wakes you. It's just Julia, standing at the foot of your bed, watching you sleep.

If you last the night, be sure to take your valuables with you when you go to breakfast. If you don't, they may be missing when you return. But don't suspect the hotel staff—it is Julia. After all, she doesn't need a key to get into your room.

Julia's tale of heartbreak is just one of many. Locals tell another enduring Santa Fe love story, about Josefina Pineda, wife of Lieutenant Rafael Pineda. Josefina and Rafael loved to dance, and even after their two daughters were born, the couple continued to attend every fandango held in Santa Fe.

But one terrible day, wounded soldiers returned from the Battle of Glorieta to tell Josefina that her husband was missing in action. They did not know if Rafael was killed or not.

Josefina was distraught. She waited and waited, but Rafael didn't return. She traveled to the battlefield and searched for his body but never found it. Many fallen soldiers had been hastily buried without a marker, and many others' remains were discovered years later in gullies and behind bushes.

Josefina plummeted into hopelessness. In her desperation, she convinced herself that if she danced, Rafael would hear her and return. Josefina attended every fandango in the city for many years, even when she was old.

One day, when Josefina was in her eighties, she visited a dance hall. When the music started, she dropped her cane and danced as if she were twenty years old. And the people in the hall reported she was not dancing alone.

The ghost of Rafael strode onto the dance floor in his dashing uniform and danced with Josefina. When the music finished, Josefina fell in a heap on the floor. She had died and gone on to her eternal rest, where she and Rafael could dance in each other's arms for eternity.

The dance hall where Josefina met her beloved husband again was located near Burro Alley, a colorful and charming part of Santa Fe's history. Come to Burro Alley late at night, when you will hear hands clapping, fingers

snapping, and feet stomping to the beat of an unheard tune. It is Josefina and Rafael, dancing an eternal fandango.

Another well-known figure haunts Burro Alley: María Gertrudis Barceló, who is more commonly known as La Tules. Tules is the Spanish word for reeds. Some believe she was called La Tules because of her slim figure. However, Tules is also a nickname for Gertrudis.

La Tules came to Santa Fe as a rich widow. She had lost her children and husband in an epidemic, so she sold all her property and came to Santa Fe to start over. La Tules played the harp and sang so well, people called her

La Ángel. She was very popular, and before long, she built a fancy entertainment hall. She imported chandeliers and enormous mirrors from St. Louis over the Santa Fe Trail. She covered the dirt floor with the finest carpets. She offered music, dancing, food, drinks, gambling, and other entertainment.

La Tules was a town leader and devout Catholic. She was a talented musician, spoke four languages, and was a successful businesswoman. She was a skilled Monte dealer. (Monte is a gambling card game that was very popular in Mexico and New Mexico.) She smoked. Spanish women at the time were encouraged to be and do all these things, if they wished. But the American women who were settling in Santa Fe thought La Tules was scandalous.

The American women disapproved of a

woman who could take care of herself and do anything a man could do. La Tules was the butt of ugly gossip, but those who knew her, like the governor of New Mexico and the bishop of Santa Fe, appreciated her.

La Tules is an inspiring woman who was an important figure in Santa Fe in the early 1800s. And she still is today. Her entertainment hall

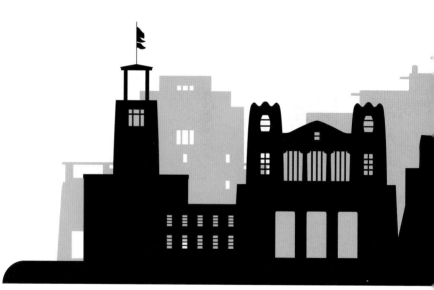

may be long gone, but if you sit on a bench in the Plaza on a warm evening, you will hear the sweet sounds of La Tules singing and strumming her harp, like an angel. And if you are brave enough to venture back down Burro Alley, listen for the sounds of clinking glasses, playing cards being shuffled, and as always, dance music.

CHAPTER 7

La Huesuda Comes

When you visit Santa Fe, learn a lesson from Tranquilino Ronquillo and bring a large pack of spearmint gum with you. You probably won't need it, but if you do . . . better safe than sorry.

Tranquilino Ronquillo was a bronco buster, cattle roper, and buffalo hunter who lived in Santa Fe. His name means mild snorer. But his snoring was not mild. In fact, he snored so long and so loud, his nickname was Morti, short for

Mortificador, which means one who bothers others. It is said that Morti's snoring was so annoying, it kept away the angel of death, La Huesuda, which means "the bony one."

Morti was good-looking and had unusual, emerald-green eyes. People found him pleasant and friendly. He danced wildly and sang loudly at the local fandangos. He wore black, even though he wasn't in mourning, which is a sure way to get La Huesuda's attention. But Morti was not afraid of anything, plus he had a special gift.

Very special.

He knew everyone's secrets. When Morti talked to someone, he instantly knew the things that no one else could—he knew the things the person had thought. The things the person had seen. Even the things the person had done. How would you feel if you met someone who could read your mind? Would it frighten you, or would you think it was a fun trick? You might think people avoided Morti so they could keep their secrets safe, but they didn't. They liked him and enjoyed his company.

But how did Morti know so much? Where did his gift come from? The answer is a little spooky. Morti believed he had lived before. In fact, he believed he had lived *many* times, dying and living over and over again. It is said that during a previous lifetime, he'd asked La Huesuda to let him live forever. La Huesuda said she would give Morti a chance to live a little longer, but not forever. She left to help other people pass into death. When she came back for Morti, she was surprised to learn that he had found a way to avoid her skeletal embrace. For a while.

Morti had two interesting habits. First, he loved to chew trementina. Trementina is sap from the piñon tree. Local people chewed trementina like chewing gum. At first, it makes your teeth stick together. But if you keep chewing, the trementina becomes more like gum. Trementina does not taste sweet, but the locals added spearmint to it, which made their breath smell good.

Morti's other interesting habit was not nearly as pleasant. He liked to drink blood. In the old days in Santa Fe, some traditional dishes were blood pudding and fried blood served with salt on a tortilla. Morti noticed that when he ate such dishes, he grew stronger and more powerful. He began to crave raw meat and whenever a cow or buffalo was slaughtered, he drank the fresh, salty blood.

One day, Morti felt tired and weak. He looked in the mirror, but he did not see his reflection. He was invisible! How could this be? He could feel his hands ... he could feel his feet ... but he could not see himself in the mirror. His mother came into the room, looking for him. She couldn't see Morti either—he was truly invisible! He thought he must be dead! Morti suddenly felt himself shooting through a dark tunnel toward a bright light, and then just as suddenly, he felt himself back in his own home.

Morti realized La Huesuda had come calling, but he had avoided her embrace this time. He knew that if he wanted to evade death, he would have to keep eating raw meat and drinking fresh blood, or he would fade out of this world. According to local legend, from that time on, Morti kept a wooden box, which he cooled with a block of ice and filled with fresh blood to keep him strong and in this world.

However, his tricks eventually caught up with him. Drinking so much blood made him smell like death, and that attracted La Huesuda. Whenever Morti heard La Huesuda's rattling bones at the foot of his bed at night, he quickly started chewing spearmint trementina. The aroma of spearmint confused her, and she went away.

But La Huesuda would not stay away forever. Death comes to everyone, even Morti. Late one night, Morti awoke because the broken clock on his wall suddenly began to chime at a quarter to midnight.

His time was running out.

Morti's many lives flashed before his eyes. He saw exciting things he had done and sad things he had endured. He saw hard times he had lived through and prosperous times he had enjoyed. He saw people he had known and loved throughout his many lives.

He lit a candle and prayed.

When the clock chimed midnight, La Huesuda appeared with her long, black robe draped over her bony form. Her hood hung eerily over her white skull. She stared at Morti with cold, sunken eyes, and he shivered in fear. La Huesuda stretched her skeletal fingers

toward him. He prayed harder and harder until finally—

—a smile played across his face. Peace overcame him, and Morti died. His soul was

saved. All across Santa Fe, all the candles blew out. Morti had finally passed on.

But the people of Santa Fe still remember Morti. He is hard to forget because they still hear his loud snores in the middle of the night. Stay in one of the homes or hotels around the Plaza and you may hear him, too. But be warned, he may not be alone. He might bring La Huesuda with him! If you hear the rattle of ancient bones, chew a little spearmint gum to confuse La Huesuda, and she will leave you alone—perhaps . . .

The Desperate Outlaw

The man reread the letter his love, Paulita, had sent: "Autumn winds are sighing; autumn flowers are dying. Sad my heart is crying, crying for your love."

He couldn't wait any longer. He lay on a bare cot in the Lincoln County Jail, waiting to be hanged. He'd gotten mixed up in a land dispute between his boss and other ranchers. When his boss was killed, the man joined a posse. The posse killed the outlaws who had murdered the man's boss. Now, the man would pay for that revenge with his life.

That man was Billy the Kid.

Billy had sent many letters to the governor of New Mexico, begging to talk to him. He had proof that the local law enforcement was crooked, and Billy thought he shouldn't be hanged for killing crooked men. The governor had promised Billy a pardon, but then, he broke his promise.

Billy was in despair. Not only was he afraid for his life; he was going to lose his love, Paulita Maxwell. He made a desperate decision. He would break out of jail.

The two men guarding Billy were notorious killers, so Billy did not hesitate. While one of the guards was taking some prisoners to dinner across the street, Billy asked to use the outhouse. (In those days, there was no indoor plumbing. People had to use a toilet in a small room built outside the building.) As Billy walked with the guard back to his cell, he slipped his thin wrist through the handcuffs and grabbed the guard's gun. Billy shot him, and when the second guard came running to see what was going on, Billy shot him, too.

Now Billy was free. But where would he run? His mother was dead. His brother had disappeared into the West. He chose to run to the only person he truly trusted in the world: Paulita Maxwell.

Paulita was the daughter of a wealthy family. She had met Billy at a fandango. Billy was known among the ladies as a gentleman who treated women well. He was an expert dancer and took great pride in his appearance when he socialized.

Paulita's brother, however, was not fond of Billy the Kid. Billy was poor. He was uneducated. He had no family. He made his living cowboying and gambling. And he was always getting into scrapes with the law. The final straw was Billy's sentence to be hanged

for murder. When Billy showed up at the Maxwell family compound, Paulita's brother got word to Sheriff Pat Garrett.

Sheriff Pat Garret had once been a friend of Billy's, but Billy was in too much trouble this time. Garrett snuck into the Maxwell house. Billy had gone to visit the outhouse, and when he came back into Paulita's bedroom, Garret was hiding behind a couch. Garrett surprised Billy and shot him straight through the heart. Billy died instantly.

But that is not the end of the story.

For many years, people claimed to see Billy the Kid in places where he used to hang out. Billy had once been in jail in Las Vegas, New Mexico (a town located east of Santa Fe and founded seventy years before the more famous Las Vegas, Nevada). Many swore they still saw him strolling the town's dusty streets. They claimed to see him in Anton Chico, a town about eighty-five miles

southeast of Santa Fe, where Billy cut a dashing figure at the fandangos. In Santa Fe and other towns, they claimed to see him playing at the card tables. And of course, his shadow is often seen around the Lincoln County Jail. Many claim to hear chains rattling in the empty cell where Billy stayed.

Today, Billy's restless spirit is still hanging around in Santa Fe. Some claim to hear the jangle of his spurs and a soft laugh, as if Billy

is enjoying a private joke. Others claim to meet a dusty cowboy who flashes a crooked, buck-toothed smile, leaning against the adobe wall of a side street. And if you spend enough time on the porch of the Palace of the Governors, you may bump into a man wearing his best suit who asks you to direct him to the governor. After all these years, Billy is *still* fighting to get his promised pardon.

A Cemetery and a Miracle

When you visit the Public Employees Retirement Association (PERA) building on Paseo de Peralta in Santa Fe, stay out of the basement. Unless you want your hair to stand on end.

The area where the building and parking lot stand has been witness to misery and death for over four hundred years. It was once the San

Miguel Church Cemetery and had been the final resting place for the people of Santa Fe since 1610. When the bishop wanted to build a boarding school for boys two hundred and fifty years later, he decided to build it partly where the old cemetery stood. Even though the workers protested, he ordered them to build the boarding school on top of the old graves.

We do not know whether the boys who attended the boarding school had ghostly experiences. But with two hundred and fifty years of death buried under the rooms where they learned, played, and slept, surely, they had eerie encounters.

Today, the PERA building sits on the same spot as the boarding school. It has a basement and a subbasement. Many old graves were disturbed when the building foundation was dug. Some graves were moved, but many were simply left in place and covered up. Some of the coffins may have even belonged to boys who died tragically at the boarding school.

Today, employees who work in the building report very strange (and very spooky!) experiences. They hear knocks at doors leading to empty storage rooms. Unearthly moans and groans echo through the halls and raise the hair on the back of their necks. And everyone avoids going to the basement at *all* costs. (Too many have felt spirit hands shoving them or phantom feet tripping them on the stairs.)

About twenty-five years after the school was founded, a terrible epidemic swept through the student body. Some say it was cholera, an intestinal infection that killed many people in the 1800s. Cholera spreads quickly when the water supply is contaminated. That's why many pioneers died of cholera on the trail. The priests who ran the school knew they had to bury their dead students quickly to keep the disease from spreading. The boys were buried in unmarked graves.

The students at the boarding school came from all over the New Mexico Territory, and the boys' parents tragically did not hear about their children's illness until they were dead and buried. One of the boys' mothers, Doña María Sanchez, rushed to Santa Fe. She demanded to know where her son was buried—but no one could tell her. The bodies had been buried in such a hurry, no one was sure who was buried where. Doña María wanted to disinter—or dig up—her son's remains and take them home for burial. But because the authorities could not

be sure which remains belonged to her son, they didn't let her.

Doña María would not leave Santa Fe without her son, so she never left at all. Day after day, she was seen praying with her rosary at San Miguel Church and sorrowfully walking around the adobe walls of the cemetery where her son was buried.

It seems Doña María still mourns her poor, dead son today. At least one janitor at the PERA building has quit rather than face seeing her ghost again. Employees often see the petite woman dressed all in black, a mantilla drawn tightly around her face. (A mantilla is a traditional lace or silk veil Mexican women often wore, and sometimes still wear when they go to church.)

Doña María walks around the PERA building, candle in hand, crying as though her heart is breaking: "*¡Mi hijo, mi pobre* *hijo!"* Which means, "My son, my poor son!" Witnesses say she disappears through walls, and can even be seen crossing the parking lot, where the bodies of many people of old Santa Fe remain buried. If you run into Doña María, don't be afraid. Offer to light a candle and say a prayer in memory of her son.

A few years after the devastating cholera outbreak, the Sisters of Loretto built a beautiful chapel meant to look like a European church, which is very different from the adobe buildings in Santa Fe. Tragedy struck, however, and the architect died before he could design a staircase that would lead to the choir loft. The workers did not have the skills to design such a staircase, and they suggested the nuns instead climb a ladder to get into the loft.

Nuns at that time wore outfits called habits, which were long, layered capes and skirts. They wore veils that covered their hair. They wore belts and rosaries. It was highly impractical to expect nuns to climb up and down a ladder to get to the choir loft on a daily basis.

So, the sisters prayed a novena to Saint Joseph. A novena is a series of prayers that is recited for nine days. On the ninth day of the nuns' novena, an old, bearded man appeared with his burro, a hammer, and a carpenter's square. The sisters wondered—could this man be the answer to their prayers? He offered to solve their problem, so they hired him.

The man worked for months, keeping his work hidden from the nuns. Finally, one day, he disappeared. When the nuns checked inside the church to see what had been going on for all those months, they were astonished. The man had built a spiral staircase

with two complete, 360-degree turns. But the amazing part was that no one could tell what was holding up the staircase. It was built like a spring. The man did not use any nails—he only used wooden pegs. And even more amazing, he had used wood from trees that did not grow anywhere near Santa Fe.

The mysterious man had not stayed to receive the nuns' thanks. He did not stay to receive payment, either. The nuns thought he must have opened an account at a lumber yard for supplies—at least they could pay *that* bill. But when they checked with all the lumber yards in town, they could find no account in their name. No one knew anything about a mysterious old man with a burro.

He had completely vanished. The nuns did not know where he came from or where he went. They decided the man who had come in answer to their prayers must have been St. Joseph himself.

Come to Loretto Chapel and marvel at the Miracle Staircase. It is beautiful, and it is still standing, though no one really knows how. Then ask yourself: Who could have built such a wonderful staircase with only a hammer and a carpenter's square? Some skeptical people believe the man was simply a skilled artisan from Mexico. Some believe he was a ghost, wandering the world, helping people. Others believe he was an angel, and some—like the nuns who received an answer to their prayer—believe it was St. Joseph, the carpenter.

What do you believe?

Lisha Cauthen lives in Kansas City at the other end of the Santa Fe Trail—she can see it from the attic in her one-hundred-year-old house. She doesn't mind the phantom footsteps she hears at night, but she does get irritated when someone invisible blows on her neck. She is an editor and writes children's books including *You Are Here*, a nonfiction picture book about space. You can learn more about Lisha at www.lishacauthen.com.

Check out some of the other *Spooky America* titles available now!

Spooky America was adapted from the creeptastic *Haunted America* series for adults. *Haunted America* explores historical haunts in cities and regions across America. Here's more from the original *Haunted Santa Fe* author Ray John de Aragón: